Motivational

AND

Inspirational Saying

Coloring Books

This book belongs to :

____

Color Testing

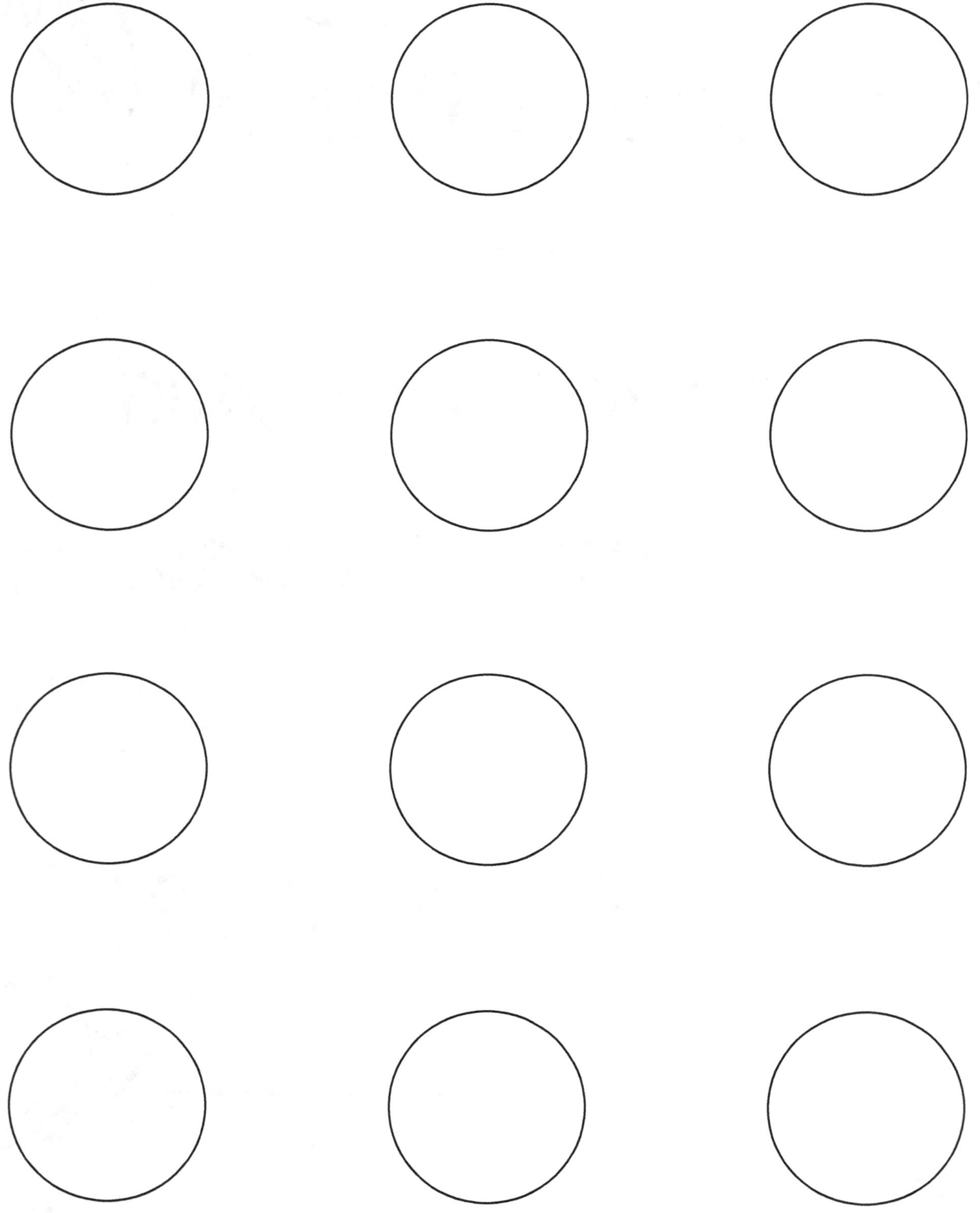

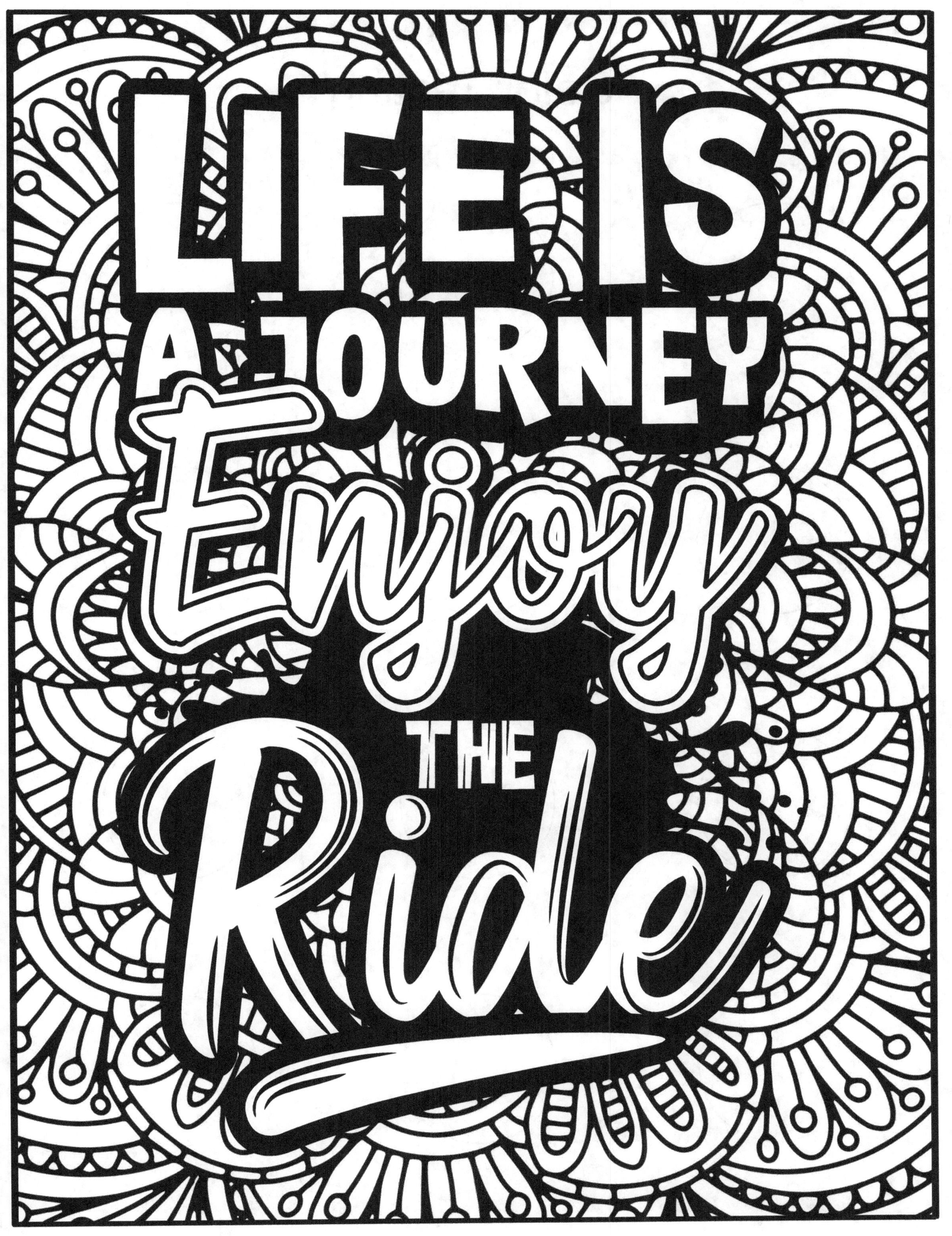

LIFE IS
A JOURNEY
Enjoy
THE
Ride

Color Testing

Allah
LISTEN TO
FOR YOU
Trust
HIM

Color Testing

Color Testing

IT'S TIME
to
Believe
IN YOU

Color Testing

MOVE
YOUR
LIFE

Color Testing

Learn
Something
New
Everyday

Color Testing

Start
EACH DAY
with a
Grateful
heart

Color Testing

Magic
is
something
you make

Color Testing

EVERY
THING
STARTS WITH A
DREAM

Color Testing

IF YOU
never try
you will
NEVER
KNOW

Color Testing

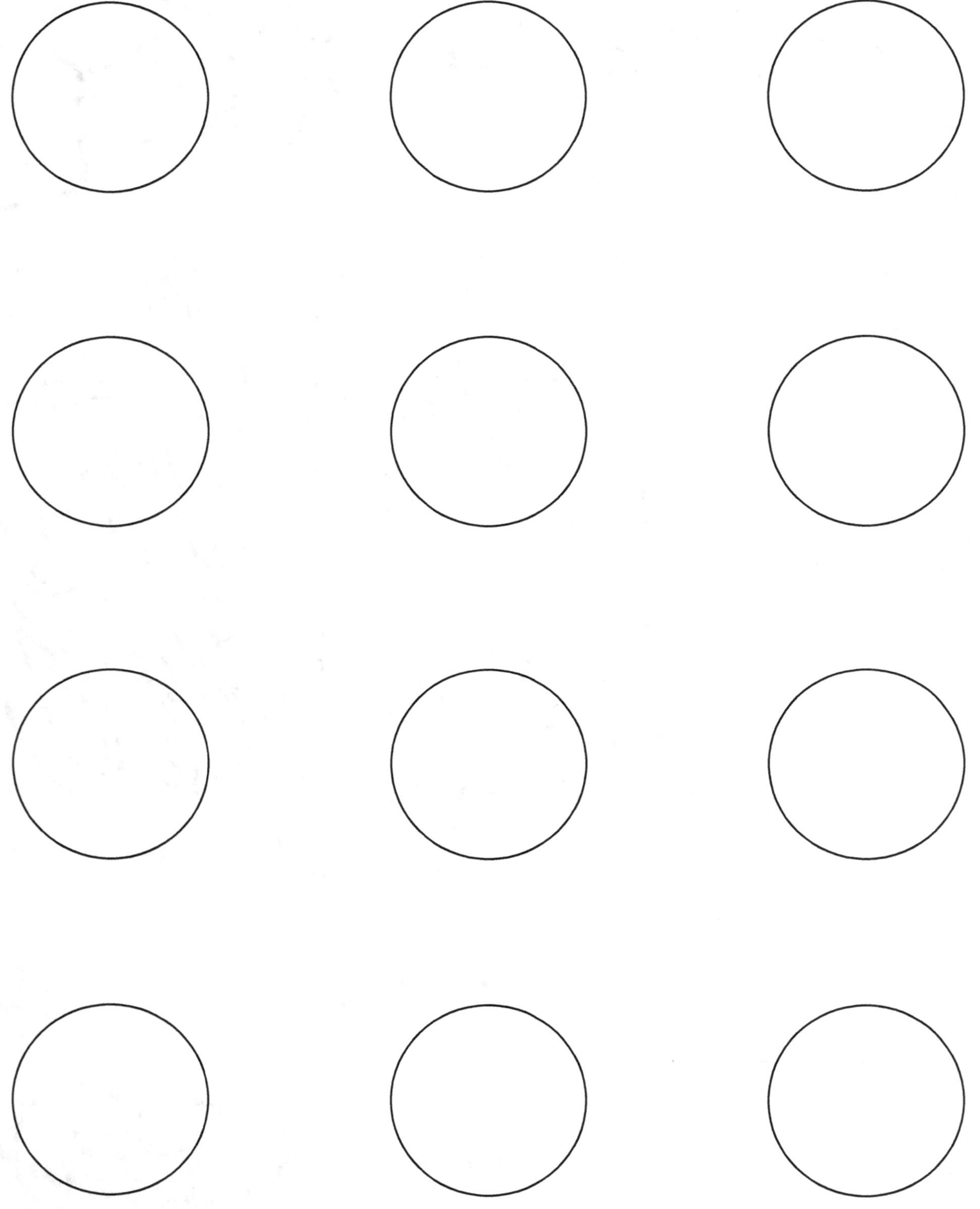

A Journey
of a
Thousand
Begins miles
with a
SINGLE
step

Color Testing

LIFE
LAUGH
LOVE

Color Testing

believe
IN
yourself

Color Testing

the
MAGIC
is in
YOU

Color Testing

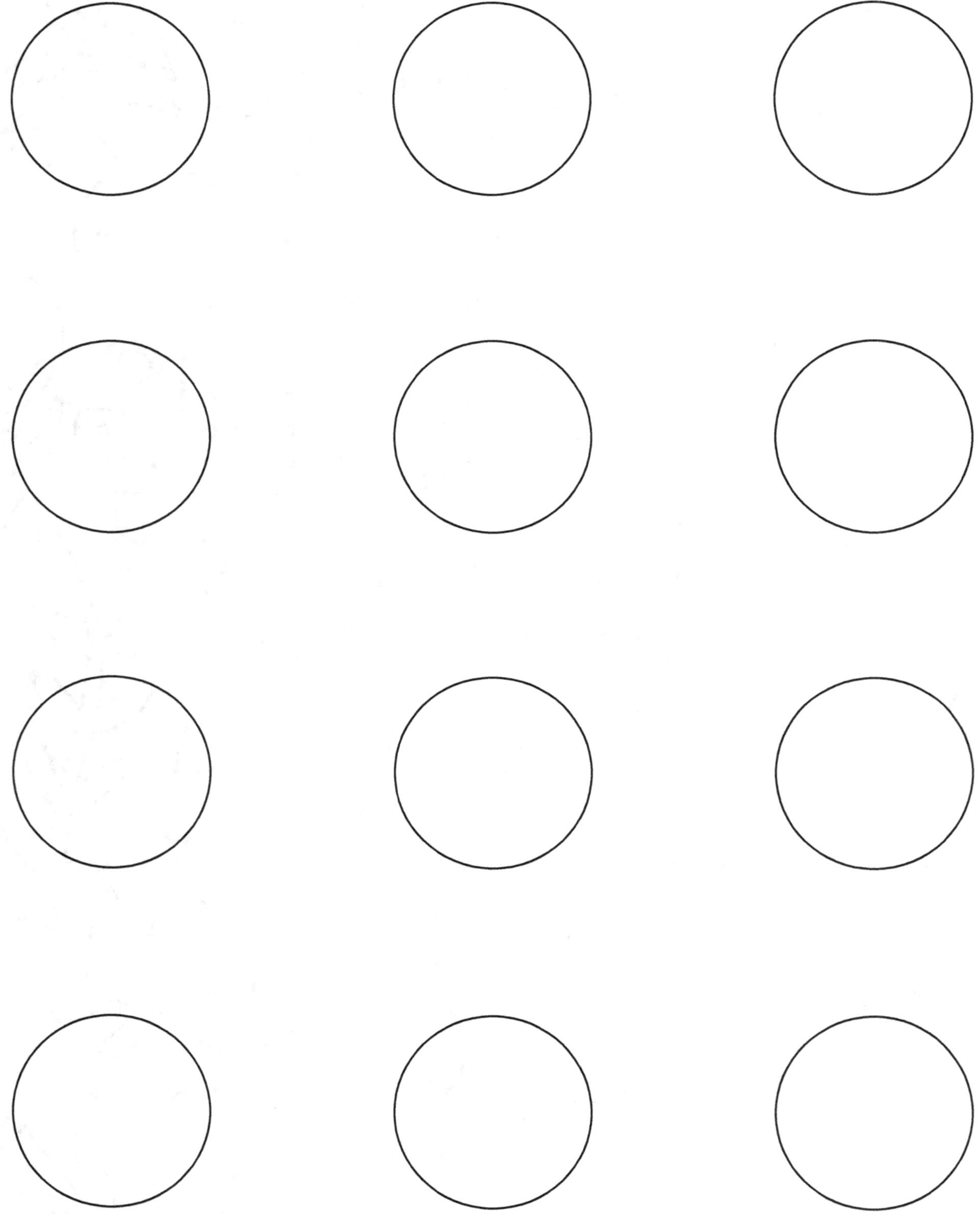

BE
Yourself
EVEN
Though
It's
DIFFERENT

Color Testing

WORK HARD IN Silence LET YOUR Success BE YOUR NOISE

Color Testing

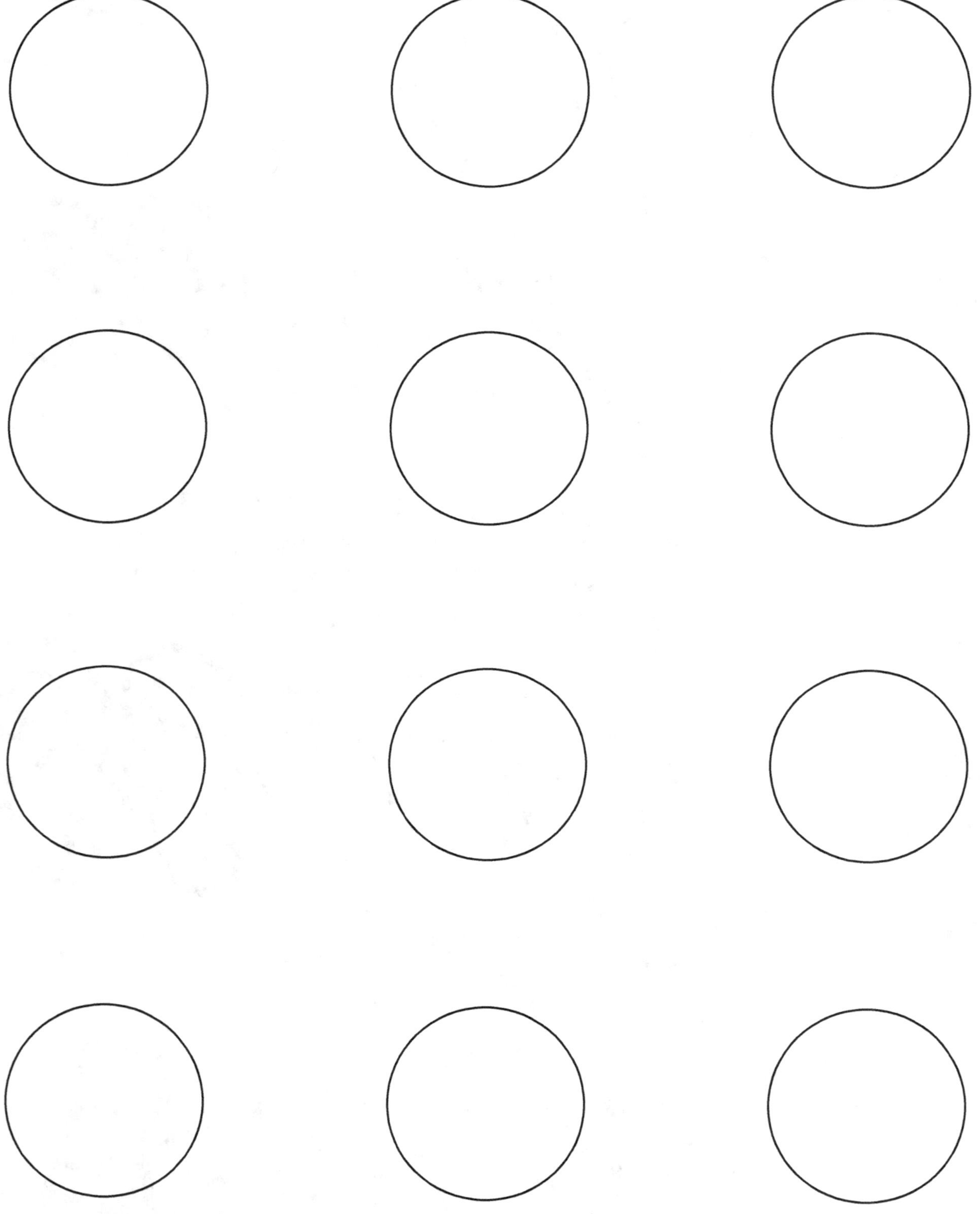

We're
Better
TOGETHER

Color Testing

Love
isn't finding
someone
You can live
with
it's finding
someone you
can't live
Without

Color Testing

thankful
grateful
blessed

Color Testing

NOBODY CAN DO IT FOR YOU
YOU HAVE TO DO IT YOURSELF

Color Testing

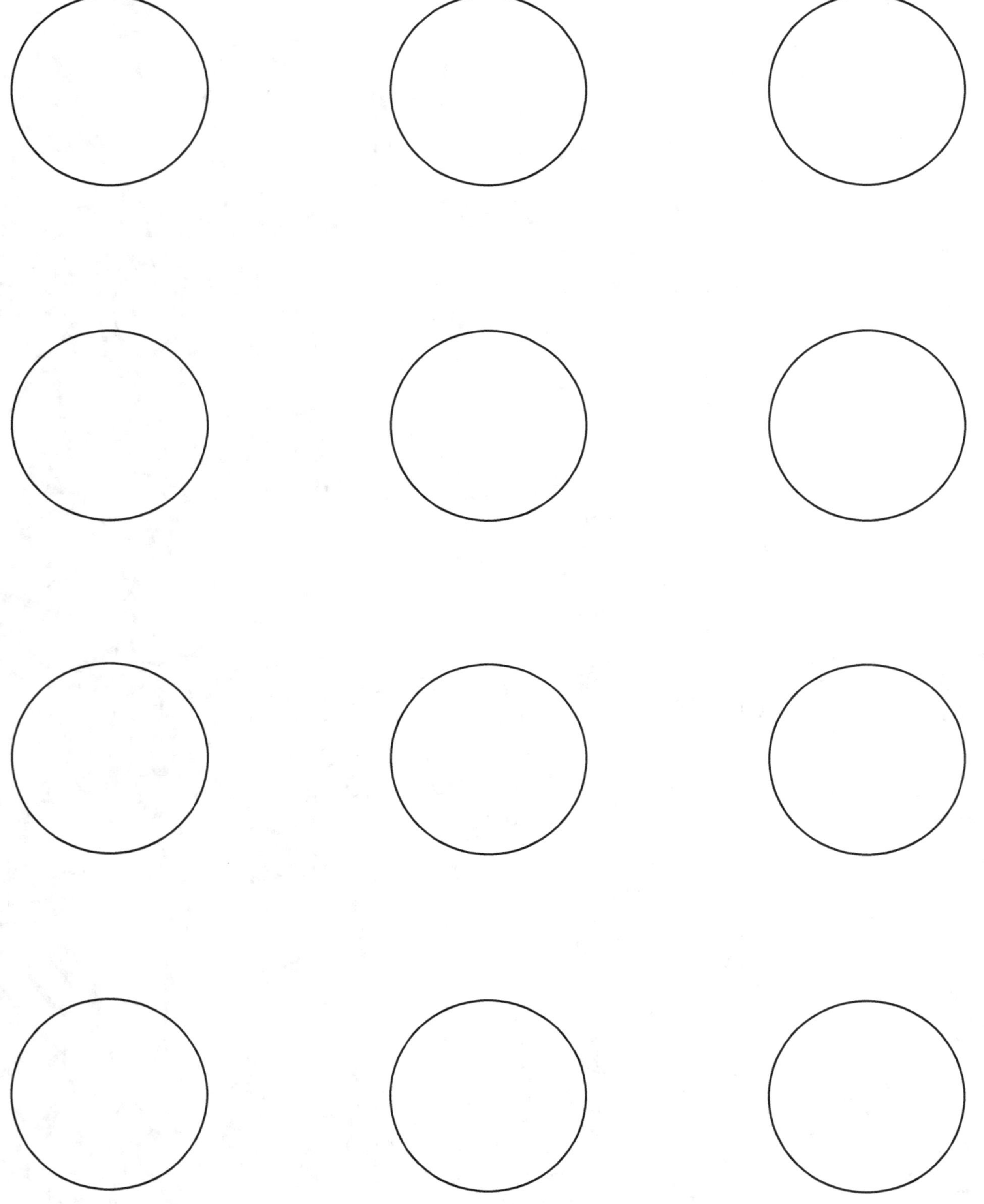

Never Stop Dreaming

Color Testing

Stop
wishing
start
Doing

Color Testing

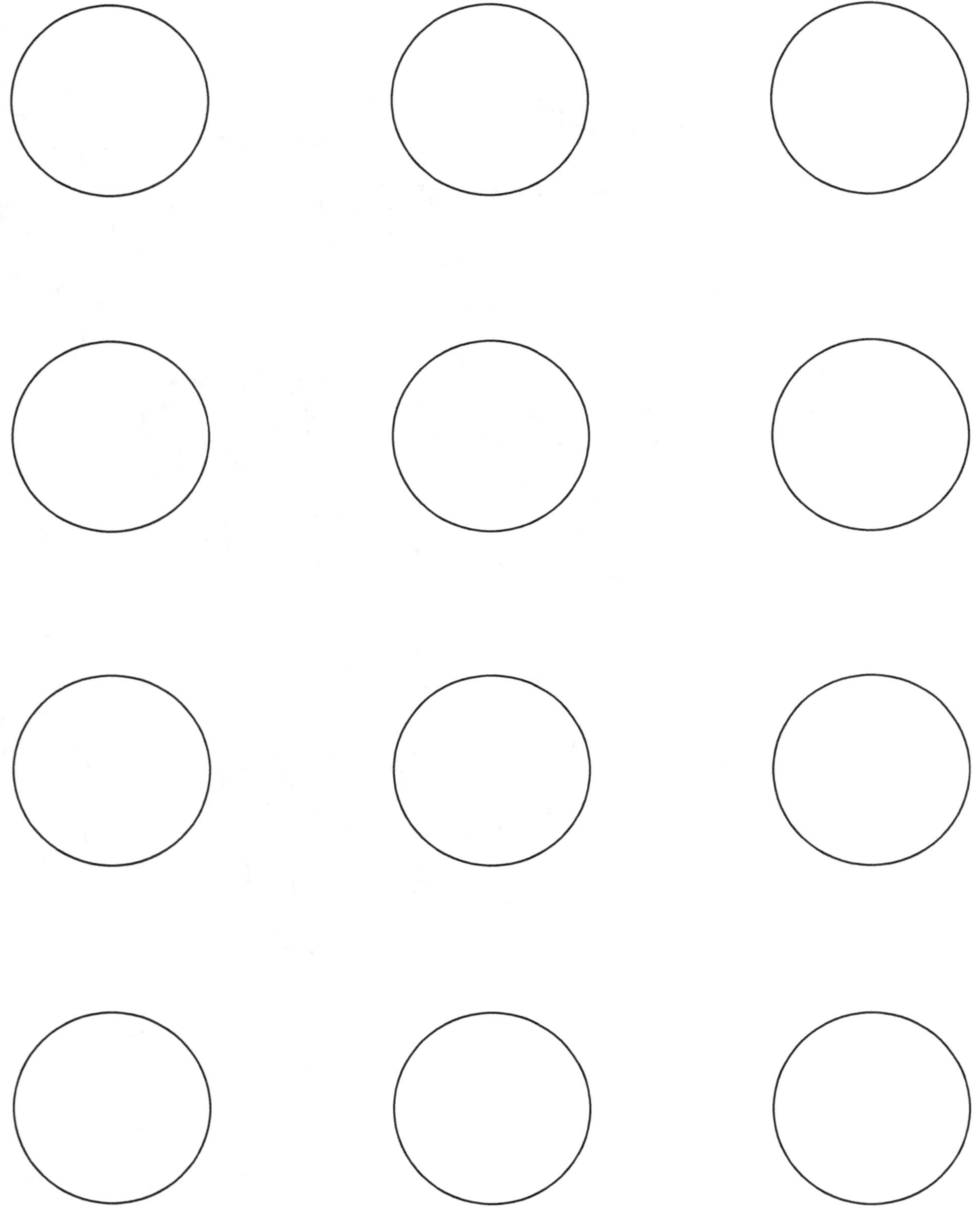

If you never try you never know

Color Testing

Let your
DREAMS
be your
Wings

Color Testing

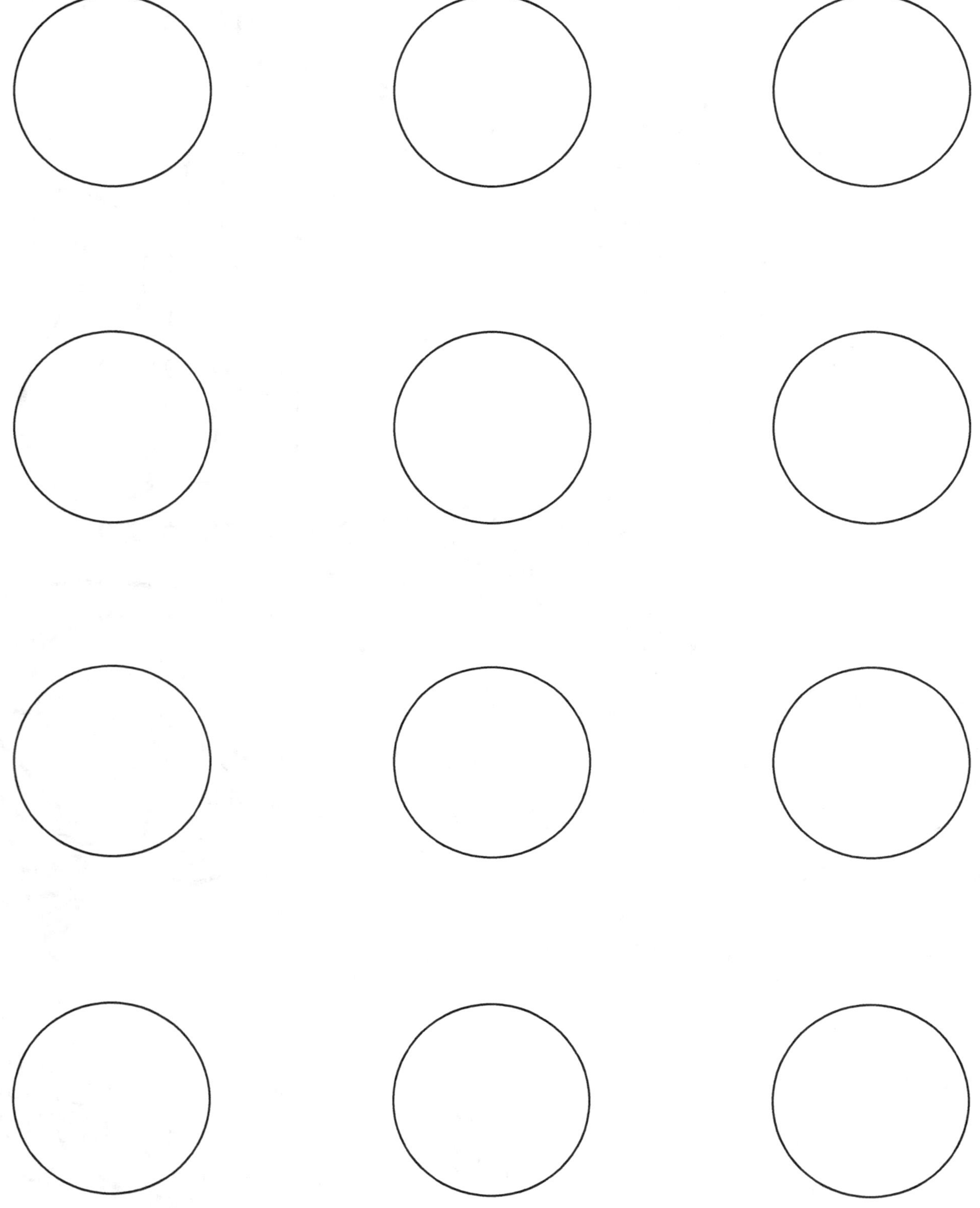

Keep
going
Keep
growing

Color Testing

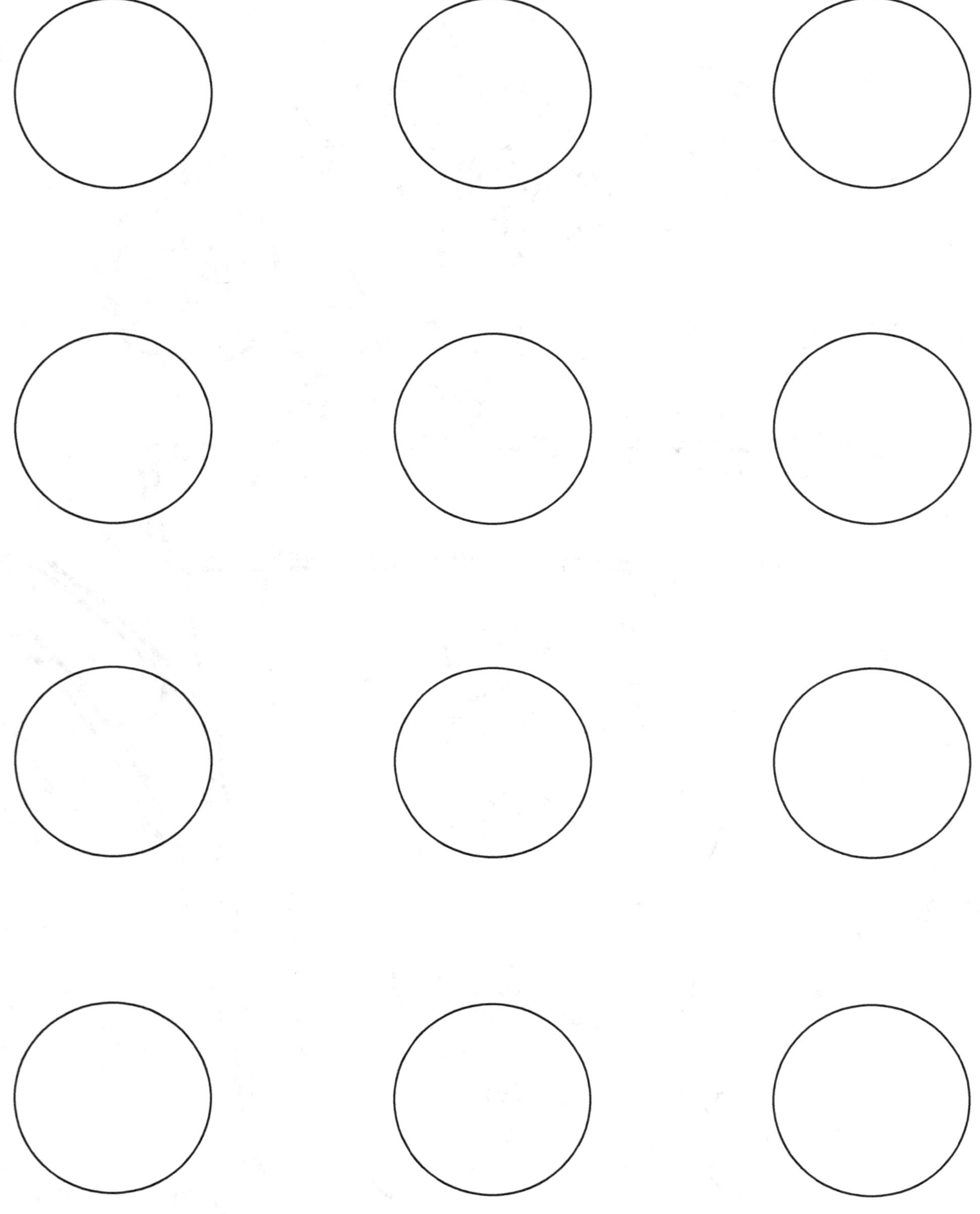

THINK
HAPPY
BE Happy

Color Testing

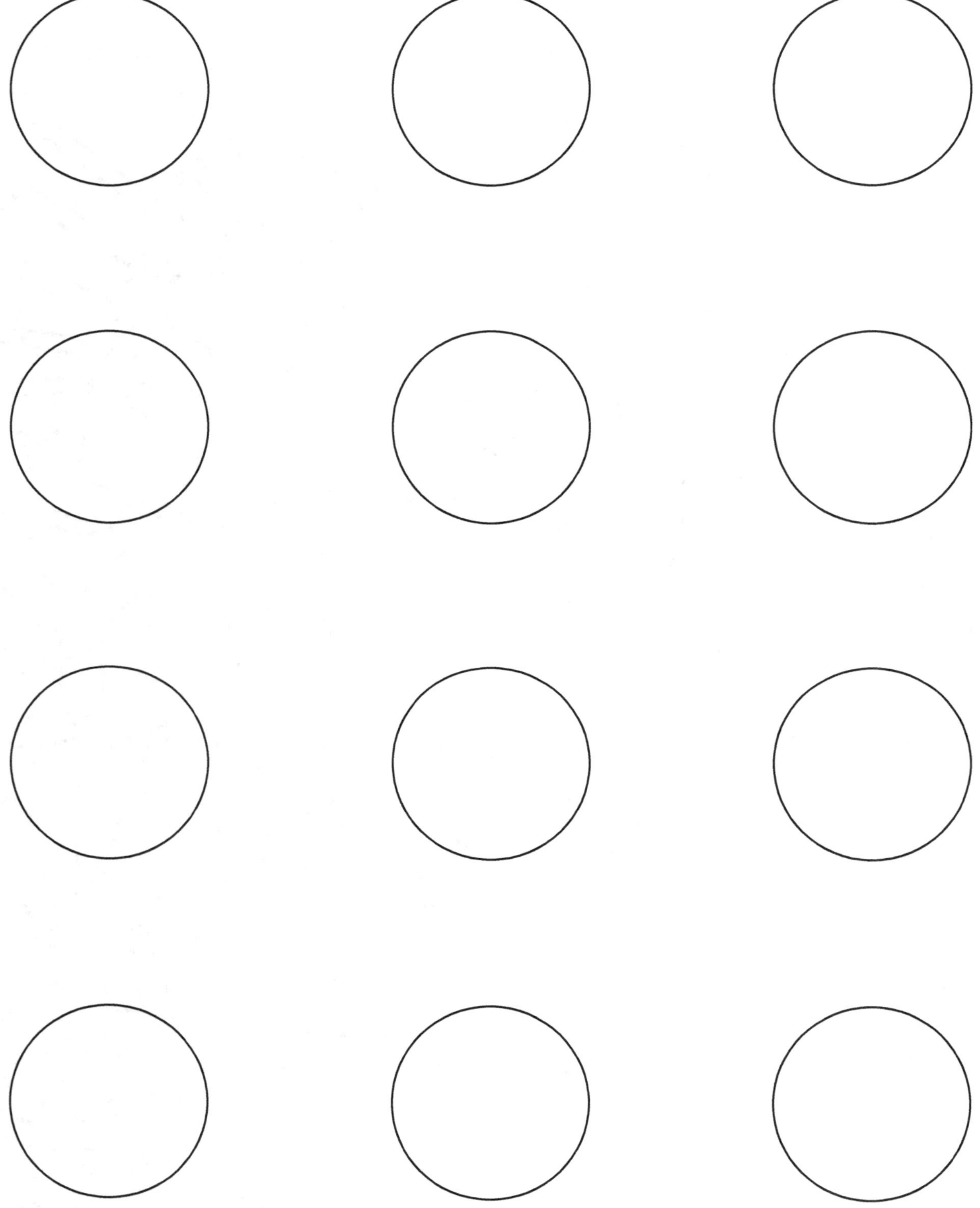

live
more
worry
less

Color Testing

ACTUALLY
I Can

Color Testing

ALWAYS
Believe
IN
YOURSELF

Color Testing

Everything
will
be Ok

www.ingramcontent.com/pod-product-compliance
Lightning Source LLC
Chambersburg PA
CBHW081428250726
48654CB00013B/1863